Pizza

Cookbook

D1715887

Introduction

Pizza seems to be more American than apple pie. Every state seems to have their own version of this delicious cheesy treat. Schools have pizza days. socialites have pizza parties and everyone seems to have a preference for their own toppings.

Enjoy a mouthwatering variety every day of the year and you will still not exhaust the endless options available. This cookbook will help you find the type that is right for you. From deep dish to thin crust, Chicago style to New York.

There is a pizza recipe for everyone.

Chicago Deep-Dish Pizza

Ingredients:

For the Dough:
1 1/3 cups warm water
2 1/4 tsps. active dry yeast
1/4 cup olive oil
1/4 cup melted butter
2 tsps. white sugar
1 1/2 tsps. fine salt
1/2 cup cornmeal
3 3/4 cups all-purpose flour
2 tsps. olive oil, or as needed, divided
4 cups pizza sauce, or to taste
For the Fillings/Toppings (in Order of Application):
4 oz. sliced provolone cheese
8 oz. fresh mozzarella cheese, cubed
1 pound spicy Italian sausage, casings removed
4 oz. shredded part-skim, low-moisture mozzarella cheese
2 oz. Parmigiano-Reggiano cheese
1 tbsp. olive oil

Directions:

1. Pour water into the bowl of a stand mixer fitted with a paddle attachment.
2. Sprinkle in yeast and let dissolve, about 10 minutes.
3. Add olive oil, melted butter, sugar, salt, cornmeal, and most of the flour.
4. Knead, stopping to scrape down the sides occasionally and adding more flour as needed, until smooth and elastic.
5. Transfer dough to a lightly floured work surface. Knead in extra flour if needed.
6. Roll into a ball and place in a bowl greased with 1/2 tsp. olive oil.
7. Cover with a plate and let rise in a warm spot until doubled in volume, 1 to 2 hours.
8. Meanwhile, let pizza sauce simmer in a pot over low heat until very thick, 60 to 90 minutes.
9. Preheat the oven to 425 degrees F (220 degrees C).
10. Poke dough to deflate and turn out onto your work surface.
11. Press and stretch out dough into a round shape 3 to 4 inches larger than a 12-inch cast iron skillet.
12. Brush skillet with 1 1/2 tsps. olive oil.
13. Place dough in the skillet; stretch and pull to evenly distribute it over the bottom and sides.

14. Lay provolone cheese over the bottom of the crust. Scatter fresh mozzarella on top.
15. Add Italian sausage and firm mozzarella. Ladle pizza sauce generously on top. Grate Parmesan cheese on top.
16. Fold the edges of the crust in towards the center to seal in the sides. Drizzle crust and center with 1 tbsp. olive oil.
17. Bake in the center of the preheated oven until crust sounds hollow and pizza is beautifully browned, about 35 minutes.
18. Let rest for 10 minutes before slicing.

Chicago Deep Dish Pizza Dough

Ingredients:

2 1/4 tsps. active dry yeast
1 1/2 tsps. white sugar
1 1/8 cups warm water - 110 to 115 degrees F (43 to 45 degrees C)
3 cups all-purpose flour
1/2 cup corn oil
1 1/2 tsps. kosher salt

Directions:

1. Dissolve yeast and sugar in warm water in a bowl. Let stand for 5 to 10 minutes until the yeast softens and begins to form a creamy foam.
2. Combine yeast mixture, flour, corn oil, and kosher salt in a large stand mixer with a hook attachment; knead until dough holds together but is still slightly sticky, about 2 minutes.
3. Form dough into a ball and transfer to a buttered bowl, turning to coat.
4. Cover bowl with a towel and allow dough to rise at room temperature until double in size, 6 hours.
5. Punch down dough and let rest for 10 to 15 minutes. Press dough into a 10-inch deep dish pizza pan.

Double Crust Stuffed Pizza

Ingredients:

1 1/2 tsps. white sugar
1 cup warm water (100 degrees F/40 degrees C)
1 1/2 tsps. active dry yeast
1 tbsp. olive oil
1/2 tsp. salt
2 cups all-purpose flour
1 (8 oz.) can crushed tomatoes
1 tbsp. packed brown sugar
1/2 tsp. garlic powder
1 tsp. olive oil
1/2 tsp. salt
3 cups shredded mozzarella cheese, divided
1/2 pound bulk Italian sausage
1 (4 oz.) package sliced pepperoni
1 (8 oz.) package sliced fresh mushrooms
1/2 green bell pepper, chopped
1/2 red bell pepper, chopped

Directions:

1. Combine the white sugar and the warm water in a large bowl or in the work bowl of a stand mixer.
2. Sprinkle the yeast over the warm sugar water, and let stand for 5 minutes until the yeast softens and begins to form a creamy foam.
3. Stir 1 tbsp. olive oil into the yeast mixture.
4. Stir 1/2 tsp. salt into the flour.
5. Mix half of the flour mixture into the yeast water, and stir until no dry spots remain.
6. Stir in the remaining flour, a 1/2 cup at a time, mixing well after each addition.
7. When the dough has pulled together, turn it out onto a lightly floured surface and knead until smooth and elastic, about 8 minutes (or mix with dough hook in stand mixer).
8. Lightly oil a large bowl, place the dough in the bowl and turn to coat with oil.
9. Cover with a light cloth, and let rise in a warm place until doubled in volume, about 1 hour.
10. Combine the crushed tomatoes, brown sugar, garlic powder, 1 tsp. olive oil, and salt in small saucepan.
11. Cover pan, and cook over low heat until tomatoes start to break down, about 30 minutes.
12. Preheat an oven to 450 degrees F (230 degrees C). Deflate the dough and turn it out onto a lightly floured surface.

13. Cut the dough into 2 equal pieces.
14. Roll one piece into a 12 inch thin circle.
15. Roll the other half into a thicker, 9 inch circle.
16. Place the 12 inch dough round into an ungreased 9 inch springform pan.
17. Sprinkle dough with 1 cup of cheese.
18. Shape sausage into a 9 inch patty and place in pan on top of the cheese.
19. Layer pepperoni, mushrooms, green pepper, red pepper, and remaining cheese on top of sausage patty.
20. Top with the 9 inch dough round and pinch edges to seal.
21. Cut several 1/2 inch vent holes in the top crust.
22. Spread sauce evenly on the top crust, leaving a 1/2 inch border at the edges.
23. Bake pizza in the preheated oven until the crust is set, the cheese is melted, and the sausage is cooked through, 40 to 45 minutes.
24. Let hot pizza rest for 15 minutes before cutting into wedges and serving.

New York Style Pizza

Ingredients:

1 tsp. active dry yeast
2/3 cup warm water (110 degrees F/45 degrees C)
2 cups all-purpose flour
1 tsp. salt
2 tbsps. olive oil
1 (10 oz.) can tomato sauce
1 pound shredded mozzarella cheese
1/2 cup grated Romano cheese
1/4 cup chopped fresh basil
1 tbsp. dried oregano
1 tsp. red pepper flakes
2 tbsps. olive oil

Directions:

1. Sprinkle the yeast over the surface of the warm water in a large bowl. Let stand for 1 minute, then stir to dissolve.
2. Mix in the flour, salt and olive oil. When the dough is too thick to stir, turn out onto a floured surface, and knead for 5 minutes. Knead in a little more flour if the dough is too sticky.
3. Place into an oiled bowl, cover, and set aside in a warm place to rise until doubled in bulk.
4. Preheat the oven to 475 degrees F (245 degrees C).
5. If using a pizza stone, preheat it in the oven as well, setting it on the lowest shelf.
6. When the dough has risen, flatten it out on a lightly floured surface.
7. Roll or stretch out into a 12 inch circle, and place on a baking pan. If you are using a pizza stone, you may place it on a piece of parchment while preheating the stone in the oven.
8. Spread the tomato sauce evenly over the dough.
9. Sprinkle with oregano, mozzarella cheese, basil, Romano cheese and red pepper flakes.
10. Bake for 12 to 15 minutes in the preheated oven, until the bottom of the crust is browned when you lift up the edge a little, and cheese is melted and bubbly. Cool for about 5 minutes before slicing and serving.

New York Style Pizza Dough

Ingredients:

1 cup warm water
1/2 cup bread flour
1 (.25 oz.) package active dry yeast
1 1/2 tsps. white sugar
2 cups bread flour, or more as needed
3 tbsps. olive oil, divided
1 1/2 tsps. salt

Directions:

1. Combine water, 1/2 cup flour, yeast, and sugar in a bowl; stir well and let sit until mixture is foamy and bubbling, about 20 minutes.
2. Stir 2 cups flour, 2 tbsps. olive oil, and salt into yeast mixture using a wooden spoon until dough holds together; turn onto a lightly floured work surface.
3. Coat the inside of a large bowl with 2 1/2 tsps. olive oil.
4. Knead dough, adding small amounts of flour as needed, until soft and slightly sticky, about 10 minutes.
5. Form dough into a ball and place in the prepared bowl; drizzle about 1/2 tsp. olive oil over dough and spread to coat entire ball.
6. Cover bowl with a clean kitchen towel and place in a warm area of the kitchen until dough is doubled in size, about 2 hours.
7. Punch dough down and place in a large resealable plastic bag; refrigerate 8 hours to overnight. When ready to use, remove dough from refrigerator and bring to room temperature before using.

Satay Chicken Pizza

Ingredients:

1 tbsp. vegetable oil
2 skinless, boneless chicken breast halves, chopped
1 cup prepared Thai peanut sauce
1 bunch green onions, chopped
4 small (4 inch) pita breads
4 slices provolone cheese

Directions:

1. Heat oil in a skillet over high heat. Sauté chicken pieces in hot oil for 6 to 7 minutes. Do not overcook!
2. Preheat oven to 425 degrees F (220 degrees C).
3. Spoon 1/4 of peanut sauce onto each pita.
4. Sprinkle 1/4 of the browned chicken and 1/4 of the scallions on top of each.
5. Top each 'pizza' with 1 slice cheese.
6. Place on a lightly greased cookie sheet and bake in the preheated oven for 10 to 12 minutes, until the cheese is melted and bubbly.
7. Let stand for 1 to 2 minutes outside of oven before you cut with a pizza cutter.

Chicken Avocado Pizza

Ingredients:

2 avocados - peeled, pitted and diced
1 tbsp. chopped fresh cilantro
1 tbsp. fresh lime juice, or to taste
salt to taste
1 clove garlic, peeled
4 (7 inch) pre-baked pizza crusts
1 tbsp. olive oil
1 cup chopped cooked chicken breast meat
1 cup cherry tomatoes, quartered
1 cup shredded Monterey Jack cheese
1 pinch cayenne pepper

Directions:

1. Preheat your oven's broiler. If you have a pizza stone, place it in the oven while it preheats.
2. In a food processor, combine the avocados and cilantro. Puree while adding lime juice and salt to taste.
3. Cover, and set aside.
4. Slice the garlic clove in half, and rub the cut side onto the tops of the pizza crusts for flavor. Brush both sides of the crusts with olive oil.
5. Spread the avocado mixture thickly over the top of each crust, then arrange chicken and tomatoes on top.
6. Sprinkle with cheese, and season lightly with cayenne pepper.
7. Place pizzas on a baking sheet if you do not have a pizza stone.
8. Broil for about 5 minutes in the preheated oven, or until the cheese has just melted and the crust is lightly toasted.

Teriyaki Chicken Pizza

Ingredients:

1 (15 oz.) can pineapple chunks - drained with juice reserved
2 skinless, boneless chicken breast halves - cut into bite-size pieces
1 tsp. minced garlic
2 (10 oz.) cans refrigerated pizza crust dough
1 cup teriyaki sauce
1 small sweet onions, thinly sliced
1 cup shredded Cheddar cheese
1 cup crumbled feta cheese

Directions:

1. Combine reserved pineapple juice, chicken, and garlic in a small baking dish.
2. Cover, and refrigerate for 1 hour.
3. Preheat oven to 400 degrees F (200 degrees C).
4. Remove chicken from pineapple. Sauté chicken and garlic in a very hot pan, so that the chicken browns just slightly.
5. Roll out pizza dough on a 16 inch pizza pan.
6. Bake dough for approximately 7 minutes, and then remove from oven. Brush dough with a thin layer of teriyaki sauce, then a layer of the onion, and top with Cheddar cheese. Then top with chicken, reserved pineapple chunks, and feta cheese.
7. Bake for an additional 15 minutes, or until cheese is bubbly and slightly browned.

Chicken and Gorgonzola Pizza

Ingredients:

2 tbsps. olive oil
1 skinless, boneless chicken breast half
1 tbsp. dried Italian seasoning
1 onion, diced
2 cloves garlic, minced
1 (8 oz.) package sliced mushrooms
1/4 cup water
1 (10 oz.) bag washed fresh spinach
1 (12 inch) pre-baked pizza crust
1 (14 oz.) jar pizza sauce
1 tomato, sliced
4 oz. crumbled Gorgonzola cheese
4 oz. shredded mozzarella cheese

Directions:

1. Preheat oven to 450 degrees F (230 degrees C).
2. Heat olive oil in a large skillet over medium-high heat, stir in the chicken breast, and cook for a few minutes until the pieces begin to plump.
3. Stir in the Italian seasoning, onion, garlic, and mushrooms; cook and stir until the mushrooms have softened and the onion has turned translucent, 5 to 10 minutes.
4. Add the water and spinach, and cover; cook a few minutes until the spinach has wilted.
5. Place the pizza crust on a pizza pan, and spread with sauce; top with the chicken and spinach mixture.
6. Arrange the tomato slices over the pizza, then sprinkle with Gorgonzola and mozzarella cheeses.
7. Bake in preheated oven until the cheese has melted and lightly toasted, 10 to 15 minutes.

Pear and Gorgonzola Cheese Pizza

Ingredients:

1 (16 oz.) package refrigerated pizza crust dough
4 oz. sliced provolone cheese
1 Bosc pear, thinly sliced2 oz. chopped walnuts
2 1/2 oz. Gorgonzola cheese, crumbled
2 tbsps. chopped fresh chives

Directions:

1. Preheat oven to 450 degrees F (230 degrees C).
2. Place pizza crust dough on a medium baking sheet.
3. Layer with Provolone cheese.
4. Top cheese with Bosc pear slices.
5. Sprinkle with walnuts and Gorgonzola cheese.
6. Bake in the preheated oven 8 to 10 minutes, or until cheese is melted and crust is lightly browned.
7. Remove from heat.
8. Top with chives and slice to serve.

Salad Pizza

Ingredients:

1 read-made pizza crust
4 oz. mixed salad greens
10 oz. cooked, boneless chicken breast halves, diced
1/4 cup Caesar salad dressing

Directions:

1. Place the pizza shell on a pizza pan or platter and top with the greens.
2. Place the chicken over the greens and drizzle with dressing.
3. Slice and serve.

Crab Rangoon Pizza

Ingredients:

1 cup vegetable oil for frying, or as needed
4 (3.5 inch square) wonton wrappers, cut into strips
1 (16 oz.) package pizza dough
6 oz. cream cheese, softened
6 tbsps. chopped green onions, divided
1/4 cup shredded Parmesan cheese, divided
4 oz. frozen crab meat, thawed
4 oz. shredded mozzarella cheese
2 tbsps. sweet chili sauce

Directions:

1. Heat vegetable oil in a deep skillet over medium-high heat; fry wonton strips until crisp, 2 to 4 minutes.
2. Transfer to a paper towel-lined plate to drain.
3. Preheat oven to 450 degrees F (230 degrees C).
4. Spread pizza dough onto a baking sheet.
5. Bake in the preheated oven until slightly brown, about 7 minutes.
6. Mix cream cheese, 1/4 cup green onions, 2 tbsps. Parmesan cheese, and crab together in a bowl.
7. Spread onto the pizza crust.
8. Top with mozzarella cheese, remaining Parmesan cheese, fried wonton strips, and remaining green onions.
9. Bake in the preheated oven until cheese is browned and melted, about 8 minutes.
10. Drizzle sweet chili sauce over top.

Grilled Zucchini Pizza

Ingredients:

1 large zucchini
1/2 cup butter, melted
3 cloves crushed garlic
1/2 cup mozzarella cheese
1/2 (14 oz.) can pizza sauce

Directions:

1. Slice the zucchini into thick rounds.
2. Combine the melted butter and crushed garlic in a small bowl. set aside.
3. When the coals on your barbeque are almost burned down, lay your zucchini slices on the grill. Let cook for three minutes then turn over and brush the butter/garlic mixture on each slice.
4. Cook for three more minutes and turn over again and brush the other side with the garlic and butter.
5. Cover the slices with pizza sauce and cheese and let cook until the cheese begins to melt.

Bacon-Artichoke Cauliflower Pizza

Ingredients:

1 frozen cauliflower pizza crust
2 tbsps. tomato sauce with oregano and basil
1/4 cup shredded mozzarella cheese
1/4 cup shredded provolone cheese
8 cherry tomatoes, halved
1/3 cup chopped sweet onion
1/3 cup fresh spinach
1/4 cup chopped black olives
3 marinated artichoke hearts, drained and chopped
2 cooked bacon strips, chopped
2 mushrooms, chopped

Directions:

1. Place a pizza stone in the oven and preheat to 425 degrees F (220 degrees C).
2. Place pizza crust on a sheet of parchment paper.
3. Top with tomato sauce.
4. Mix mozzarella and provolone cheeses together and sprinkle 1/4 cup over the pizza.
5. Layer cherry tomatoes, onion, spinach, black olives, artichokes, bacon, and mushrooms on top.
6. Sprinkle remaining 1/4 cup cheese on top.
7. Slide pizza onto the hot pizza stone.
8. Bake until crispy and golden brown, 13 to 15 minutes.
9. Remove from the oven, slice, and serve.

BBQ Chicken Pizza

Ingredients:

1 (12 inch) pre-baked pizza crust
1 cup spicy barbeque sauce
2 skinless boneless chicken breast halves, cooked and cubed
1/2 cup chopped fresh cilantro
1 cup sliced pepperoncini peppers
1 cup chopped red onion
2 cups shredded Colby-Monterey Jack cheese

Directions:

1. Preheat oven to 350 degrees F (175 degrees C).
2. Place pizza crust on a medium baking sheet.
3. Spread the crust with barbeque sauce.
4. Top with chicken, cilantro, pepperoncini peppers, onion, and cheese.
5. Bake in the preheated oven for 15 minutes, or until cheese is melted and bubbly.

Goat Cheese Pizza

Ingredients:

1 (11 oz.) log goat cheese, crumbled
1 (7 oz.) jar roasted red peppers, drained and chopped
1 cup chopped sun-dried tomatoes marinated in olive oil, drained
4 pita bread rounds
1 cup fresh basil leaves, torn
1/2 cup balsamic vinegar

Directions:

1. Preheat the oven to 400 degrees F (200 degrees C).
2. Separate the pita breads by cutting around the outer edge, and carefully prying the halves apart to make two rounds out of each one.
3. Place the separated pita rounds onto cookie sheets.
4. Generously sprinkle goat cheese, roasted red peppers and sun-dried tomatoes onto each one.
5. Bake the pizzas for 16 minutes in the preheated oven, or until the crust is crisp. As soon as the pizzas come out of the oven, sprinkle with torn basil, and drizzle with balsamic vinegar.
6. Cut into quarters, and serve hot or warm.

Brussels Sprouts Pizza

Ingredients:

1 tsp. extra-virgin olive oil
9 slices pancetta
5 tsps. extra-virgin olive oil
2 cloves garlic, minced
6 Brussels sprouts, trimmed and thinly sliced
1 (8 oz.) package shredded mozzarella cheese
1/2 tsp. fennel seed
1 12-inch pizza crust

Directions:

1. Preheat oven to 475 degrees F (245 degrees C).
2. Heat 1 tsp. olive oil in a skillet over medium heat; cook and stir pancetta until fat has been released, 3 to 5 minutes.
3. Transfer pancetta to a paper towel-lined plate.
4. Pour remaining 5 tsps. olive oil into the same skillet; cook and stir garlic until fragrant, about 20 seconds.
5. Add Brussels sprouts to garlic; cook, stirring constantly, until sprouts begin to brown, 5 to 10 minutes.
6. Transfer sprouts and garlic to a bowl and crumble cooled pancetta over the mixture.
7. Add mozzarella cheese and fennel seed; toss to coat.
8. Place pizza crust onto a baking sheet and spread Brussels sprouts mixture atop pizza crust.
9. Bake in the preheated oven until cheese is melted and bubbling, about 10 minutes.

Muffaletta Pizza

Ingredients:

8 jumbo black olives, pitted
8 pitted green olives
2 tbsps. chopped celery
2 tbsps. chopped red onion
2 cloves chopped garlic
6 leaves chopped fresh basil
1 tbsp. chopped fresh parsley
2 tbsps. olive oil
1/2 tsp. dried oregano
Salt and freshly ground black pepper to taste
1 (16 oz.) package ready-made pizza crust
1 tbsp. olive oil
1/2 tsp. garlic powder to taste
Salt to taste
2 oz. shredded mozzarella cheese
2 oz. shredded provolone cheese
2 oz. grated Parmesan cheese
2 oz. thinly sliced hard salami, cut into strips
2 oz. thinly sliced mortadella, cut into strips
4 oz. thinly sliced prosciutto, cut into strips

Directions:

1. In a medium bowl, mix jumbo black olives, green olives, celery, red onion, garlic, basil, parsley, olive oil, oregano, salt and freshly ground black pepper.
2. Cover and chill in the refrigerator until using.
3. Preheat oven to 500 degrees F (260 degrees C).
4. Sprinkle pizza crust with olive oil, salt and garlic powder.
5. Place the crust directly on the oven rack.
6. Bake for about 5 minutes. Do not allow crust to become overly browned or crisp.
7. Remove from heat and allow to cool.
8. In a medium bowl, mix together mozzarella cheese, Provolone cheese, Parmesan cheese, hard salami, mortadella and prosciutto.
9. Stir in the olive mixture.
10. Preheat the broiler.
11. Spread the cheese and vegetable mixture over the baked pizza crust.
12. Broil 5 minutes, or until cheeses are melted and meats are lightly browned.
13. Cut into 3 inch squares and serve immediately.

Reuben Pizza

Ingredients:

1 (1 pound) loaf frozen whole wheat bread dough, thawed
1/2 cup thousand island dressing
2 cups shredded Swiss cheese
6 oz. deli sliced corned beef, cut into strips
1 cup sauerkraut - rinsed and drained
1/2 tsp. caraway seed
1/4 cup chopped dill pickles

Directions:

1. Preheat the oven to 375 degrees F (190 degrees C).
2. Grease a large pizza pan. On a lightly floured surface, roll the bread dough out into a large circle about 14 inches across.
3. Transfer to the prepared pizza pan. Build up the edges, and prick the center all over with a fork so it doesn't form a dome when baking .
4. Bake for 20 to 25 minutes in the preheated oven, or until golden.
5. Spread half of the salad dressing over the hot crust.
6. Sprinkle with half of the Swiss cheese.
7. Arrange corned beef over the cheese, then drizzle with the remaining salad dressing.
8. Top with sauerkraut and remaining Swiss cheese.
9. Sprinkle with caraway seed.
10. Bake for another 10 minutes in the preheated oven, until cheese melts and toppings are heated through.
11. Sprinkle with chopped pickle. Let stand for 5 minutes before slicing.

Fruit Pizza

Ingredients:

1 (16.5 oz.) package refrigerated sliceable sugar cookies, sliced
1 (8 oz.) package cream cheese, softened
1/4 cup sugar
1/2 tsp. vanilla
4 cups assorted cut-up fruit (kiwi, strawberries, blueberries, drained canned mandarin oranges)
1/4 cup apricot preserves, pressed through sieve to remove lumps
1 tbsp. water

Directions:

1. Heat oven to 375 degrees F.
2. Line 12-inch pizza pan with foil; spray with cooking spray.
3. Arrange cookie dough slices in single layer in prepared pan; press together to form crust.
4. Bake 14 min.; cool completely. Invert onto plate; carefully remove foil. Turn crust over.
5. Beat cream cheese, sugar and vanilla with mixer until well blended.
6. Spread over crust.
7. Top with fruit.
8. Mix preserves and water; brush over fruit. Refrigerate 2 hours.

BBQ Pulled Pork Pizza

Ingredients:

1 (14 oz.) package pre-baked pizza crust
2 tbsps. barbeque sauce
1 tsp. chipotle chili powder
Salt and ground black pepper to taste
1/2 cup prepared pulled pork
1/8 cup sliced onion
1/8 cup sliced red bell pepper

Directions:

1. Preheat oven to 450 degrees F (230 degrees C).
2. Place the pizza crust onto a baking sheet.
3. In a bowl, mix the barbeque sauce with chipotle chili powder; season with salt and black pepper.
4. Spread the sauce over the pizza crust.
5. Arrange pulled pork, sliced onion, and red bell pepper slices evenly over the pizza.
6. Bake in the preheated oven until the toppings are hot and the pizza crust is crisp on the bottom, 12 to 15 minutes.

Scrambled Egg Pizza

Ingredients:

2/3 cup warm water
1 (.25 oz.) package instant yeast
1/2 tsp. salt
1 tsp. white sugar
1/4 tsp. dried oregano
1 3/4 cups all-purpose flour
6 slices bacon, chopped
1/2 cup green onion, thinly sliced
6 eggs, beaten
Salt and pepper to taste
1/2 cup pizza sauce
1/4 cup grated Parmesan cheese
2 oz. thinly sliced salami

Directions:

1. Preheat oven to 400 degrees F (200 degrees C).
2. Pour warm water into a mixing bowl.
3. Stir in yeast, salt, sugar, and oregano.
4. Mix in 1 cup flour, and then stir in remaining flour.
5. Cover with plastic wrap, and set aside to rest for 10 to 15 minutes.
6. While dough is resting, prepare topping.
7. Place bacon in a large, deep skillet.
8. Cook over medium heat until evenly brown.
9. Stir in green onions, and cook for 1 minute.
10. Add eggs to the pan; cook, stirring frequently, until mixture has the consistency of scrambled eggs.
11. Season with salt and pepper to taste.
12. Spread dough out evenly onto a lightly greased pizza tray, and spread pizza sauce over dough.
13. Top with bacon and eggs, Parmesan cheese, and salami.
14. Bake for 20 to 25 minutes, or until golden brown on top.

Brie and Cranberry Pizza

Ingredients:

1 (8 oz.) can refrigerated crescent rolls
8 oz. cubed Brie cheese
3/4 cup whole berry cranberry sauce
1/2 cup chopped pecans

Directions:

1. Preheat oven to 425 degrees F (220 degrees C).
2. Lightly grease a 12 inch pizza pan or 9x13 inch baking dish.
1. Unroll the crescent rolls and separate into triangles.
2. Arrange in the pan with tips towards the center and lightly press together.
3. Bake 5 minutes, or until lightly brown.
4. Remove from the oven and sprinkle with pieces of Brie cheese. Spoon the cranberry sauce over the cheese.
5. Top with pecans.
6. Bake an additional 8 minutes, or until the cheese is melted and the crust is golden brown. Cool 5 minutes and cut into wedges or squares.

Brie Cranberry and Chicken Pizza

Ingredients:

2 skinless, boneless chicken breast halves
1 tbsp. vegetable oil
1 (12 inch) prepared pizza crust
1 1/2 cups cranberry sauce
6 oz. Brie cheese, chopped
8 oz. shredded mozzarella cheese

Directions:

1. Preheat oven to 350 degrees F (175 degrees C).
2. Chop chicken breasts into bite-size pieces.
3. Heat oil in medium skillet until hot.
4. Add chicken and sauté until browned and almost cooked through.
5. Spread cranberry sauce over the pizza crust.
6. Top with chicken, brie and cover with mozzarella.
7. Bake at 350 degrees F (175 degrees C) for 20 minutes.

Hawaiian Pizza

Ingredients:

1 (13.8 oz.) package refrigerated pizza crust dough
6 strips turkey bacon or lean deli ham slices
1 cup pizza sauce
1 1/2 cups shredded mozzarella cheese
1 (20 oz.) can pineapple chunks, drained
1/2 cup thinly sliced green or red bell pepper strips
1/4 cup sliced green onion or diced red onion
2 tbsps. chopped cilantro (optional)

Directions:

1. Preheat oven to 400 degrees F. Spray a large baking sheet with non-stick cooking spray. Press dough into a 15 x 10-inch rectangle, and decoratively pinch the edges, if desired.
2. Bake 8 to 10 minutes or until edges begin to turn light golden brown.
3. Meanwhile, cook bacon or deli ham until crisp in a non-stick skillet over medium-high heat; crumble and set aside.
4. Spread pizza sauce evenly over crust.
5. Sprinkle with cheese and remaining toppings.
6. Bake 10 to 15 minutes or until cheese is melted and crust is golden brown.

Smoked Salmon Pizza

Ingredients:

1 (12 inch) pre-baked pizza crust
1 tbsp. olive oil
1 cup smoked salmon, cut into 1/2 inch pieces
1/2 (6 oz.) jar marinated artichoke hearts, drained and quartered
2 tbsps. chopped sun-dried tomatoes
2 cups shredded mozzarella cheese

Directions:

1. Preheat an oven to 400 degrees F (200 degrees C).
2. Spread the olive oil over the pizza crust, then sprinkle with the smoked salmon, artichokes, and sun-dried tomatoes.
3. Sprinkle the mozzarella cheese evenly over the pizza.
4. Bake in the preheated oven until the cheese has melted and is bubbly, 10 to 15 minutes.

Fresh Tomato and Basil Pizza

Ingredients:

1 pound refrigerated pizza dough
1 tbsp. olive oil
1 (8 oz.) package shredded Mozzarella cheese, divided
3 cups cherry tomatoes, halved
1 cup loosely packed fresh basil leaves, torn
Freshly ground black pepper

Directions:

1. Heat oven to 500 degrees F.
2. Pat and stretch dough into 14x6-inch rustic rectangle on baking sheet sprayed with cooking spray; brush with oil.
3. Top with 1 cup cheese.
4. Combine tomatoes, basil and pepper; spread over pizza.
5. Top with remaining cheese.
6. Bake 12 to 15 min. or until crust is golden brown.

Ham, Asparagus, and Ricotta Pizza

Ingredients:

1 cup fresh asparagus, trimmed
1/2 cup ricotta cheese
1/4 cup olive oil
2 cloves garlic, minced
1 pinch red pepper flakes, or to taste
Salt and freshly ground black pepper to taste
2 tbsps. heavy cream
2 tbsps. chopped herbs, such as basil, parsley, rosemary, thyme
1 pound pizza dough
1 tbsp. flour, for dusting
1/2 cup diced smoked ham
1/2 cup shredded sharp white Cheddar cheese
1 tbsp. finely grated Parmigiano-Reggiano cheese

Directions:

1. Preheat an oven to 550 degrees F (285 degrees C).
2. Bring a large pot of lightly salted water to a boil.
3. Add asparagus and cook uncovered until just tender, about 2 minutes.
4. Drain in a colander, then immediately immerse in ice water for several minutes. Once asparagus is cold, drain well and set aside.
5. Combine ricotta, olive oil, garlic, red pepper flakes, salt, black pepper, and heavy cream in a small bowl.
6. Stir in fresh herbs (if using) and set aside.
7. To shape the pizza dough, sprinkle the countertop and dough surface with flour and lightly pat flat. Use a rolling pin to form a thin disk about 9 inches in diameter. Transfer to a baking sheet.
8. Spread ricotta mixture over crust, top with ham and asparagus.
9. Sprinkle with Cheddar and Parmigiano-Reggiano cheeses.
10. Place baking sheet on the bottom rack of the preheated oven and bake for 5 minutes. Transfer the baking sheet to the top rack and bake for an additional 5 minutes.

Ham, Asparagus, and Ricotta Pizza

Ingredients:

1 cup fresh asparagus, trimmed
1/2 cup ricotta cheese
1/4 cup olive oil
2 cloves garlic, minced1 pinch red pepper flakes
Salt and freshly ground black pepper to taste
2 tbsps. heavy cream
2 tbsps. chopped herbs, such as basil, parsley, rosemary, thyme
1 pound pizza dough
1 tbsp. flour, for dusting
1/2 cup diced smoked ham
1/2 cup shredded sharp white Cheddar cheese
1 tbsp. finely grated Parmigiano-Reggiano cheese

Directions:

1. Preheat an oven to 550 degrees F (285 degrees C).
2. Bring a large pot of lightly salted water to a boil.
3. Add asparagus and cook uncovered until just tender, about 2 minutes.
4. Drain in a colander, then immediately immerse in ice water for several minutes. Once asparagus is cold, drain well and set aside.
5. Combine ricotta, olive oil, garlic, red pepper flakes, salt, black pepper, and heavy cream in a small bowl.
6. Stir in fresh herbs (if using) and set aside.
7. To shape the pizza dough, sprinkle the countertop and dough surface with flour and lightly pat flat. Use a rolling pin to form a thin disk about 9 inches in diameter. Transfer to a baking sheet.
8. Spread ricotta mixture over crust, top with ham and asparagus.
9. Sprinkle with Cheddar and Parmigiano-Reggiano cheeses.
10. Place baking sheet on the bottom rack of the preheated oven and bake for 5 minutes. Transfer the baking sheet to the top rack and bake for an additional 5 minutes.

Fried Peach and Pancetta Pizza

Ingredients:

8 oz. pancetta bacon, thickly sliced
1 tsp. olive oil, or as needed
12 oz. pizza dough, or more to taste, cut into quarters
1 tbsp. all-purpose flour, or as needed
1 cup olive oil, or as needed
1/2 cup ricotta cheese
2 tsps. chopped fresh thyme, or to taste
Ground black pepper to taste
20 slices fresh peach
1/4 cup freshly grated Parmigiano-Reggiano cheese
4 tsps. extra-virgin olive oil, or to taste

Directions:

1. Preheat an oven to 475 degrees F (245 degrees C). Line baking sheets with aluminum foil.
2. Sprinkle pancetta into a cold skillet and drizzle 1 tsp. olive oil over pancetta.
3. Cook and stir pancetta over medium heat until browned and caramelized, 5 to 10 minutes.
4. Remove pan from heat and cool pancetta in the oil in the skillet.
5. Place 1 dough quarter on a work surface and lightly dust with flour; roll into a 1/8-inch-thick irregularly shaped crust. Stretch dough with your hands to an even thickness; let rest on the work surface for 5 minutes.
6. Repeat with remaining dough.
7. Heat about 1 cup olive oil, reaching about 1/2-inch depth, in a heavy cast iron skillet over medium-high heat.
8. Fry each piece of dough until browned and cooked through, about 2 minutes per side. The first side will be lighter than the second side.
9. Drain the crusts on paper towels.
10. Transfer pizza crusts, lighter-side up, to prepared baking sheets.
11. Spread about 2 tbsps. ricotta cheese onto each crust using the back of a spoon.
12. Sprinkle about 1/2 tsp. fresh thyme over ricotta layer.
13. Sprinkle pancetta over the ricotta-thyme layer; season with black pepper. Nestle about 5 peach slices onto each pizza, working around the pancetta pieces.
14. Sprinkle 1 tbsp. Parmesan-Reggiano cheese over each pizza. Drizzle about 1 tsp. extra-virgin olive oil over Parmesan-Reggiano layer.

15. Bake in the preheated oven until cheese is melted and peaches are lightly browned and tender, 12 to 15 minutes.
16. Cool pizzas for 5 to 10 minutes on the baking sheet.

Sriracha Honey Chicken Pizza

Ingredients:

1/2 cup honey
3 tbsps. sriracha sauce, or more to taste
2 skinless, boneless chicken breasts, cut into 3/4-inch pieces
1 (10 oz.) container refrigerated pizza crust
1/4 cup ranch dressing
1 cup Colby Jack cheese

Directions:

1. Preheat Panasonic Countertop Induction Oven to medium on the "Grill" setting.
2. Mix honey and sriracha sauce together in a bowl.
3. Spread chicken on the grill pan and set the timer for 4 minutes. Turn chicken after 2 minutes.
4. Remove from the oven and stir into the honey mixture.
5. Unroll pizza crust flat onto the grill pan.
6. Spread ranch dressing on top.
7. Remove chicken from the honey mixture and place on top of the ranch dressing.
8. Sprinkle Colby Jack cheese over chicken.
9. Place pizza in the oven and press "Auto Cook." Select the frozen pizza setting, 12-inch size. Allow pizza to cook until timer goes off, about 13 minutes.
10. Cut pizza into slices.

Campfire Pepperoni Pizza

Ingredients:

1 pound refrigerated pizza dough
1/4 cup pizza sauce
1/2 cup shredded mozzarella cheese
1/2 cup sliced pepperoni

Directions:

1. Place pizza stone on grill directly over wood fire. You may need to begin by spreading out the wood if the flames are too tall.
2. Roll out the pizza dough to desired thickness.
3. Place it on the pizza stone and cook 10 minutes on one side until golden.
4. Remove from the fire and on the cooked side, spread the pizza sauce in an even layer over dough leaving about a half inch around the rim of the pizza dough bare.
5. Sprinkle mozzarella cheese evenly on top of the sauce, followed by the pepperoni slices.
6. Place uncooked side down, back on the pizza stone.
7. Cover with a foil tent and cook until cheese has melted, about 10 minutes more. Transfer pizza to a cutting board and let cool slightly before cutting and serving.

Mediterranean Pesto Pizza

Ingredients:

2 tbsps. prepared pesto
2 (6 inch) Greek pita flatbreads
1/2 cup feta cheese
2 small tomatoes, chopped
8 pitted Kalamata olives

Directions:

1. Preheat oven to 350 degrees F (175 degrees C).
2. Spread pesto onto each pita; top with feta cheese, tomatoes, and Kalamata olives.
3. Place each pita onto a baking sheet.
4. Bake in the preheated oven until cheese is melted, 6 to 8 minutes.

Jalapeno Popper Pizza

Ingredients:

8 slices bacon, cut into 1-inch pieces
3/4 cup chopped onion
2 cloves garlic, chopped
1/2 tsp. ground cumin
1/2 tsp. dried oregano
1/2 tsp. ground black pepper
1 (8 oz.) package cream cheese, cut into cubes
1/4 cup sour cream
1 prepared 16-inch pizza dough pastry
1 cup shredded mozzarella cheese, or more to taste
1/2 cup shredded reduced-fat Cheddar cheese
4 jalapeno peppers, sliced into thin rings
1 tbsp. dried parsley flakes

Directions:

1. Preheat oven to 400 degrees F (200 degrees C).
2. Place the bacon in a large skillet and cook over medium-high heat, turning occasionally, until evenly browned, about 10 minutes.
3. Remove bacon with a slotted spoon to drain on paper towels, reserving drippings in the pan.
4. Sauté onion in bacon drippings until translucent, 5 to 7 minutes.
5. Add garlic; continue to sauté until garlic is golden, 2 to 3 minutes.
6. Season the onion mixture with cumin, oregano, and black pepper.
7. Stir cream cheese and sour cream into the onion mixture until smooth and spreadable.
8. Spread the cream cheese mixture evenly over the pizza dough; top with mozzarella and Cheddar cheeses.
9. Arrange bacon and jalapeno pepper rings over the cheese layer.
10. Sprinkle parsley over the entire pizza.
11. Bake in preheated oven until crust is firm and crispy and the cheese is browned and bubbly, about 30 minutes.

Greek Pizza

Ingredients:

1 tbsp. olive oil
1/2 cup diced onion
2 cloves garlic, minced
1/2 (10 oz.) package frozen chopped spinach, thawed and squeezed dry
1/4 cup chopped fresh basil
2 1/4 tsps. lemon juice
1 1/2 tsps. dried oregano
Ground black pepper to taste
1 (14 oz.) package refrigerated pizza crust
1 tbsp. olive oil
1 cup shredded mozzarella cheese
1 large tomato, thinly sliced
1/3 cup seasoned bread crumbs
1 cup shredded mozzarella cheese
3/4 cup crumbled feta cheese

Directions:

1. Preheat oven to 400 degrees F (200 degrees C). If using a pizza stone, place in oven to preheat.
2. Heat 1 tbsp. olive oil in a large skillet; cook and stir onion and garlic until tender, about 5 minutes.
3. Add spinach and continue to cook and stir until all liquid has evaporated, 5 to 7 minutes.
4. Remove from heat and season with basil, lemon juice, oregano, and pepper. Allow mixture to cool slightly.
5. Unroll pizza dough on preheated pizza stone or a large baking sheet and brush with remaining 1 tbsp. olive oil.
6. Spread spinach mixture over dough, leaving a small border at the edge of the pizza crust.
7. Top with 1 cup mozzarella cheese.
8. Press tomato slices into seasoned bread crumbs until coated; arrange tomatoes over pizza.
9. Spread remaining 1 cup mozzarella cheese and feta cheese over tomatoes.
10. Bake in preheated oven until pizza crust is golden brown and cheese is melted, about 15 minutes.

Taco Pizza

Ingredients:

1/2 pound ground beef
1/2 cup chopped onion
1 clove garlic
1/2 (1 oz.) packet taco seasoning mix
1/3 cup water
1 (14.5 oz.) can diced tomatoes with garlic and onion
1 cup salsa
2 tbsps. chopped fresh cilantro
1 cup refried beans
1 12-inch prepared pizza crust
1 1/2 cups Mexican shredded four-cheese blend
2 cups shredded lettuce
2 tomatoes, chopped
1 (2.25 oz.) can sliced black olives, drained
1/4 cup chopped green onion
1/2 cup Mexican-style shredded four-cheese blend
1 cup sour cream, or as desired
1 cup salsa, or as desired

Directions:

1. Cook and stir the ground beef, onion, and garlic together in a large skillet over medium-high heat until the beef is completely browned; drain fat from the skillet.
2. Stir the taco seasoning mix and water into the beef mixture; bring to a boil, reduce heat to medium-low, and cook at a simmer, stirring occasionally, for 5 minutes.
3. Preheat an oven to 350 degrees F (175 degrees C).
4. Place the prepared pizza curst on a baking sheet.
5. Blend the diced tomatoes with garlic and onion, salsa, and cilantro in a blender until smooth.
6. Spread the refried beans in an even layer on the prepared pizza crust, leaving a border of about 1/2-inch uncovered around the outside.
7. Spread about 1 cup of the diced tomato mixture over the refried beans in an even layer; reserve the remaining sauce.
8. Scatter the ground beef mixture over the layer of sauce.
9. Cover the beef with 1 1/2 cups Mexican-style shredded cheese blend.
10. Bake in the preheated oven until the cheese is bubbly and the edges of the crust are golden brown, 15 to 20 minutes.
11. Set aside to cool 5 minutes.

12. Top the pizza with shredded lettuce, chopped tomatoes, black olives, green onions, and 1/2 cup Mexican-style shredded cheese blend.
13. Serve with the reserved sauce, sour cream, and 1 cup salsa.

Veggie Pizza

Ingredients:

2 (8 oz.) packages refrigerated crescent rolls
1 cup sour cream
1 (8 oz.) package cream cheese, softened
1 tsp. dried dill weed
1/4 tsp. garlic salt
1 (1 oz.) package ranch dressing mix
1 small onion, finely chopped
1 stalk celery, thinly sliced
1/2 cup halved and thinly-sliced radishes
1 red bell pepper, chopped
1 1/2 cups fresh broccoli, chopped
1 carrot, grated

Directions:

1. Preheat oven to 350 degrees F (175 degrees C). Spray a jellyroll pan with non-stick cooking spray.
2. Pat crescent roll dough into a jellyroll pan. Let stand 5 minutes. Pierce with fork.
3. Bake for 10 minutes, let cool.
4. In a medium-sized mixing bowl, combine sour cream, cream cheese, dill weed, garlic salt and ranch dip mix.
5. Spread this mixture on top of the cooled crust.
6. Arrange the onion, carrot, celery, broccoli, radish, bell pepper and broccoli on top of the creamed mixture.
7. Cover and let chill. Once chilled, cut it into squares and serve.

Whole Wheat and Honey Pizza Dough

Ingredients:

1 (.25 oz.) package active dry yeast
1 cup warm water
2 cups whole wheat flour
1/4 cup wheat germ
1 tsp. salt
1 tbsp. honey

Directions:

1. Preheat oven to 350 degrees F (175 degrees C).
2. In a small bowl, dissolve yeast in warm water.
3. Let stand until creamy, about 10 minutes.
4. In a large bowl combine flour, wheat germ and salt.
5. Make a well in the middle and add honey and yeast mixture.
6. Stir well to combine.
7. Cover and set in a warm place to rise for a few minutes.
8. Roll dough on a floured pizza pan and poke a few holes in it with a fork.
9. Bake in preheated oven for 5 to 10 minutes, or until desired crispiness is achieved.

Hummus Pizza

Ingredients:

1 (10 oz.) can refrigerated pizza crust dough
1 cup hummus spread
1 1/2 cups sliced bell peppers, any color
1 cup broccoli florets
2 cups shredded Monterey Jack cheese

Directions:

1. Preheat the oven to 475 degrees C (220 degrees C).
2. Roll out pizza crust and place on a pizza pan or baking sheet.
3. Spread a thin layer of hummus over the crust.
4. Arrange sliced peppers and broccoli over the hummus, and top with shredded cheese.
5. Bake for 10 to 15 minutes in the preheated oven, until the crust is golden brown and cheese is melted in the center.
6. Slice and serve.

Crab Artichoke Pizza

Ingredients:

1 pound fresh pizza dough
1/4 tsp. red pepper flakes
1 (6 oz.) can crabmeat, drained and cartilage removed
1 (6 oz.) jar quartered artichoke hearts in water, drained
2 tbsps. olive oil
1 1/2 tbsps. minced garlic
1/2 cup shredded Parmesan cheese
1 cup shredded mozzarella cheese

Directions:

1. Preheat oven to 350 degrees F (175 degrees C).
2. Lightly grease a pizza pan.
3. Roll out pizza dough on a floured surface to a 14 or 16 inch circle; place onto a pizza pan.
4. Sprinkle dough with red pepper flakes, then top evenly with crab and artichokes. Drizzle with olive oil, then sprinkle with garlic, Parmesan cheese, and mozzarella cheese.
5. Bake in preheated oven until the cheese has melted and the crust is no longer doughy, about 20 minutes.
6. Set oven to broil, and cook pizza for 5 minutes more until the cheese has begun to brown.

Shrimp Pizza

Ingredients:

1 (8 oz.) package cream cheese, softened
1 cup grated Parmesan cheese
1/2 cup mayonnaise
2 cloves garlic, minced
1 (10 oz.) package frozen chopped spinach, thawed and drained
1 (10 oz.) container refrigerated pizza dough
2 tbsps. olive oil
1 tsp. Italian seasoning
2 tbsps. olive oil1 small red bell pepper, sliced
1/2 small red onion, sliced
2 tsps. Italian seasoning
2 (6.5 oz.) cans small shrimp, drained

Directions:

1. Preheat an oven to 400 degrees F (200 degrees C).
2. Stir together the cream cheese, Parmesan cheese, mayonnaise, garlic, and spinach until evenly mixed; set aside.
3. Press the pizza dough onto a baking sheet, and brush with 2 tbsps. of olive oil.
4. Sprinkle with 1 tsp. Italian seasoning.
5. Bake in the preheated oven until golden brown, 10 to 12 minutes.
6. Meanwhile, heat 2 tbsps. of olive oil in a skillet over medium heat, and cook the bell pepper and onion until tender, about 5 minutes.
7. Season with 2 tsps. of Italian seasoning, and stir in the canned shrimp; cook until the shrimp are heated through.
8. When the crust has baked, remove from the oven, and spread evenly with the spinach mixture.
9. Spread the shrimp and vegetable mixture onto the pizza, and cut into pieces to serve.

Pesto Pizza

Ingredients:

1 (12 inch) pre-baked pizza crust
1/2 cup pesto
1 ripe tomato, chopped
1/2 cup green bell pepper, chopped
1 (2 oz.) can chopped black olives, drained
1/2 small red onion, chopped
1 (4 oz.) can artichoke hearts, drained and sliced
1 cup crumbled feta cheese

Directions:

1. Preheat oven to 450 degrees F (230 degrees C).
2. Spread pesto on pizza crust.
3. Top with tomatoes, bell peppers, olives, red onions, artichoke hearts and feta cheese.
4. Bake for 8 to 10 minutes, or until cheese is melted and browned.

Eggs Benedict Breakfast Pizza

Ingredients:

12 eggs, well beaten
1 tbsp. butter
2 (8 oz.) cans refrigerated crescent rolls
1 (.9 oz.) package hollandaise sauce mix
2/3 cup milk
1/4 cup butter
3 cups diced cooked ham
1 cup shredded sharp Cheddar cheese

Directions:

1. Melt 1 tbsp. butter in a nonstick skillet over medium heat.
2. Pour in eggs, and cook to desired degree of doneness, stirring constantly.
3. Preheat an oven to 400 degrees F (200 degrees C).
4. Unroll crescent dough and place rolls on an ungreased 12 inch pizza pan with points toward the center.
5. Press seams together and press up sides of pan to form a crust.
6. Prepare Hollandaise sauce according to package directions using 2/3 cup milk and 1/4 cup butter.
7. Pour evenly over crescent roll crust.
8. Spread scrambled eggs evenly over sauce, then top with cubed ham.
9. Sprinkle lightly with shredded cheese.
10. Bake in preheated oven until bottom of crust is lightly browned, about 30 minutes.

Gourmet White Pizza

Ingredients:

2 tbsps. butter, melted
1 tbsp. olive oil
3 tbsps. minced garlic
2 tbsps. sun-dried tomato pesto
1 tsp. dried basil
1 tsp. dried oregano
1 tbsp. grated Parmesan cheese
1 cup Alfredo sauce
2 cups chopped cooked chicken breast meat
1 (12 inch) pre-baked pizza crust
1 medium tomato, sliced
1 (4 oz.) package feta cheese

Directions:

1. Preheat the oven to 375 degrees F (190 degrees C).
2. In a small bowl, mix together the butter, olive oil, garlic, pesto, basil, oregano, Parmesan cheese and Alfredo sauce.
3. Arrange the chicken on top of the pizza crust.
4. Pour the Alfredo sauce mixture evenly over the chicken.
5. Top with tomato and feta cheese.
6. Bake for 10 to 15 minutes in the preheated oven, until the crust is lightly browned and toppings are toasted.
7. Cut into wedges to serve.

Cheeseburger Pizza

Ingredients:

Nonstick cooking spray
1 (13.8 oz.) can refrigerated pizza dough
1 pound ground beef
1 onion, chopped
1 cup mayonnaise
1/3 cup prepared yellow mustard
1 1/2 cups shredded Cheddar cheese
3/4 cup chopped dill pickles

Directions:

1. Preheat the oven to 400 degrees F (200 degrees C).
2. Grease a baking sheet with nonstick cooking spray; unroll pizza dough over the baking sheet.
3. Bake in the preheated oven until golden, about 8 minutes.
4. Meanwhile, cook and stir beef and onion in a skillet over medium heat until beef is browned and crumbly, 5 to 7 minutes.
5. Drain.
6. Mix mayonnaise and mustard together in a small bowl.
7. Spread over the parbaked crust.
8. Layer beef-onion mixture, Cheddar cheese, and pickles on top.
9. Return to the oven and bake until crust is dark golden brown, 6 to 10 minutes.

Breakfast Sausage Pizza

Crust Ingredients:

1 3/4 cups all-purpose flour, or more if needed
1 envelope pizza crust yeast or rapid rise yeast
3/4 tsp. salt
2/3 cup water
1 tbsp. olive oil

Toppings Ingredients:

8 oz. sausage, cooked and crumbled
1 cup frozen hash brown potatoes, thawed
1/4 cup chopped onion
3 large eggs
1/2 tsp. ground mustard
1/2 tsp. fine grind black pepper
1/2 tsp. salt
1 cup shredded cheddar cheese

Directions:

1. Combine 1 cup flour, undissolved yeast and salt in a large bowl.
2. Heat water and oil until very warm (120 degrees to 130 degrees F).
3. Add to flour mixture and beat for 2 minutes.
4. Add enough remaining flour to make a soft dough. Knead until smooth and elastic, about 5 minutes. (If using RapidRise yeast, let dough rest at this point for 10 minutes.)
5. Roll dough to 12-inch circle; place in greased pizza pan. OR, pat dough with floured hands, pressing gently to fill greased pizza pan or baking sheet. Form a rim by pinching the edge of the dough; prick surface with fork.
6. Bake crust in preheated 450 degrees F oven on lowest oven rack for 8 minutes.
7. Reduce oven to 375 degrees F.
8. Remove pizza from oven.
9. Top pizza crust with sausage, hash browns and onions. Beat eggs, ground mustard, pepper and salt together in a bowl.
10. Pour over toppings.
11. Sprinkle with cheese.
12. Bake for 16 to 20 minutes until eggs are set and crust is browned.

Pear and Prosciutto Pizza

Ingredients:

6 cloves garlic
1/2 tbsp. olive oil
2 ripe pears, halved and cored
1 tbsp. olive oil
all-purpose flour for dusting
1 unbaked pizza crust
1 tbsp. cornmeal for dusting
6 oz. shredded Swiss cheese
5 thin slices prosciutto, cut into halves
1 (6 oz.) package fresh mozzarella, cut into small cubes
salt and ground black pepper to taste
1/2 tbsp. olive oil

Directions:

1. Preheat oven to 375 degrees F (190 degrees C).
2. Place the garlic in a small square of aluminum foil. Drizzle 1/2 tbsp. of olive oil over the garlic.
3. Wrap foil around garlic to seal.
4. Roast the garlic in the preheated oven until soft, about 20 minutes. Smash roasted cloves with a fork.
5. Place the pears in a bowl with 1 tbsp. olive oil; toss to coat.
6. Arrange pear slices on a baking sheet.
7. Bake in hot oven until soft, 10 to 15 minutes.
8. Raise oven temperature to 400 degrees F (200 degrees C).
9. Preheat a pizza stone or baking sheet in the oven.
10. Lightly dust a flat surface with flour.
11. Roll the prepared pizza crust dough out onto the prepared surface. Dust a baking sheet with cornmeal. Lay the dough onto the prepared baking sheet.
12. Spread the mashed garlic onto the dough; top with the Swiss cheese.
13. Arrange the pears, prosciutto, and mozzarella cheese onto the pizza.
14. Season with salt and pepper. Brush the edges of the crust with the 1/2 tbsp. olive oil.
15. Bake in preheated oven until the cheese is melted and crust is golden brown, 15 to 20 minutes.

S'mores Pizza

Ingredients:

1 pound refrigerated pizza dough
2 tbsps. unsalted butter, melted, divided
2 cups chopped chocolate
2 cups miniature marshmallows
3 honey graham crackers, crushed
1/4 tsp. flaky sea salt (Optional)

Directions:

1. Rest dough on a floured work surface for 20 minutes.
2. Preheat an outdoor grill for high heat and lightly oil the grate.
3. Line a baking sheet with a layer of aluminum foil. Brush a 14-inch circle on the foil using 1 tbsp. butter.
4. Roll out dough to 1/4-inch thickness on the work surface. Lay onto the buttered area of the aluminum foil.
5. Brush the top with the remaining 1 tbsp. butter.
6. Sprinkle chocolate evenly on top.
7. Spread marshmallows, graham crackers, and salt over the chocolate.
8. Slide the foil onto the grill over indirect heat.
9. Grill, lid closed, until crust is golden and marshmallows are toasted, 8 to 10 minutes.
10. Cut pizza into pieces. Cool before serving, about 5 minutes.

Pizza Margherita

Ingredients:

3 1/2 cups all-purpose flour
1 tsp. salt
1 cup water
1 (.25 oz.) package active dry yeast
1 pinch white sugar
1/4 cup flour for dusting
2 cups pizza sauce
20 slices fresh mozzarella cheese
20 leaves fresh basil
Olive oil
Sea salt to taste

Directions:

1. Stir flour and 1 tsp. salt in a bowl.
2. Set aside.
3. Mix water, yeast, and sugar in a large bowl. Let stand until yeast begins to form a creamy foam, about 5 minutes.
4. Stir half the flour mixture into yeast mixture until no dry spots remain.
5. Stir in remaining flour, 1/2 cup at a time, mixing well after each addition. When dough pulls together, turn it out onto a lightly floured surface and knead until smooth and elastic, about 8 minutes.
6. Lightly oil a large bowl, then place dough in the bowl and turn to coat with oil.
7. Cover with a light cloth and let rise in a warm place (80 to 95 degrees F (27 to 35 degrees C)) until doubled in volume, about 1 hour. Punch dough down, divide into 4 equal pieces, and form each into a ball.
8. Preheat oven with a pizza stone to 500 degrees F (260 degrees C).
9. Stretch out and pat 1 dough ball to form a circle 10 to 12 inches in diameter.
10. Place dough on a lightly floured pizza peel.
11. Top with 1/2 cup of tomato sauce and spread to cover within an inch of the edge of the dough.
12. Arrange 5 slices of mozzarella cheese on top of the tomato sauce, then place 5 basil leaves on top. Drizzle pizza with 1 tbsp. olive oil and sprinkle with sea salt to taste.
13. Repeat for 3 remaining dough balls.
14. Slide each pizza onto the pizza stone in the preheated oven.
15. Bake until cheese is bubbly and the underside of the crust is golden brown, 5 to 7 minutes.

Homemade Pepperoni Pizza

Pizza Sauce Ingredients:

1/2 (12 oz.) can tomato paste
1 tsp. dried oregano, crushed
1 tsp. dried basil, crushed
1/2 tsp. garlic powder
1/2 tsp. onion powder
1/2 tsp. sugar
1/2 tsp. salt
1/4 tsp. black pepper

Pizza Crust Ingredients:

3 1/4 cups all-purpose flour, or more as needed
2 (.25 oz.) envelopes pizza crust yeast or rapid rise yeast
1 tbsp. sugar
1 1/2 tsps. salt
1 1/3 cups very warm water (120 degrees F to 130 degrees F)
1/3 cups oil

Sauce Directions:

1. Combine all sauce ingredients with 1/2 cup water in a medium bowl; set aside for flavors to develop while making crust.
2. Freeze remaining paste.

Crust Directions:

1. Combine 2 cups of flour with the dry yeast, sugar and salt.
1. Add the water and oil and mix until well blended (about 1 minute).
2. Gradually add enough remaining flour slowly, until a soft, sticky dough ball is formed.
3. Knead for about 4 minutes, on a floured surface, until dough is smooth and elastic.
4. Add more flour, if needed.
5. If using rapid rise yeast, let dough rest, covered, for 10 minutes.
6. Divide dough in half. Pat each half (with floured hands) into a 12-inch greased pizza pan OR roll dough to fit pans.
7. For pizzas: Preheat oven to 425 degrees F.
8. Top crusts with sauce, pepperoni and cheese.
9. Bake for 18 to 20 minutes until crusts are browned and cheese is bubbly.
10. For best results, rotate pizza pans between top and bottom oven racks halfway through baking.

Poutine Pizza

Ingredients:

2 cups all-purpose flour
1 cup lukewarm water
1 egg
1 tbsp. instant yeast
1 tbsp. white sugar
1 (14 oz.) package frozen French fries
cooking spray
10 slices bacon, chopped
1 (12 oz.) bag shredded Mexican cheese blend
1/2 cup pizza sauce, or as needed
1 (10.5 oz.) can beef gravy, or as needed

Directions:

1. Place flour in a large bowl.
2. Whisk water, egg, yeast, and sugar together in a cup.
3. Make a well in the flour and pour in yeast mixture.
4. Stir until mixture forms a smooth dough, adding a small amount of flour or water if needed.
5. Cover bowl with a towel; set aside to rise until doubled in size, about 30 minutes.
6. Preheat oven to 425 degrees F (220 degrees C).
7. Spread French fries in a single layer on a baking sheet.
8. Bake fries in the preheated oven until golden, about 20 minutes.
9. Reduce oven temperature to 350 degrees F (175 degrees C).
10. Heat a large skillet over medium heat and fry bacon pieces until browned, about 5 minutes; remove to drain on a paper towel.
11. Spray a round pizza pan with baking spray.
12. Punch down dough, and flatten onto pizza pan.
13. For a stuffed crust, sprinkle about 1/4 cup shredded Mexican cheese blend around the edge of the dough, roll dough inward over cheese, and pinch dough to seal.
14. Spread a thin layer of pizza sauce over dough.
15. Spread fries over dough; pour gravy over fries as needed to cover.
16. Top with remaining Mexican cheese blend.
17. Sprinkle bacon pieces evenly over pizza.
18. Bake in the preheated oven until cheese is bubbly and crust is golden, about 20 minutes.

Beer Pizza

Ingredients:

1 tbsp. olive oil
1/2 pound pepperoni sausage, diced
1 pound bacon, diced
1 (4 oz.) can sliced mushrooms, drained
1 onion, chopped
1 green bell pepper, chopped
1 (28 oz.) can tomato sauce
1 cup beer
1 clove garlic, minced
1 tsp. dried oregano
1/2 tsp. dried thyme
1/2 tsp. salt
2 unbaked pizza crusts
1 (8 oz.) package shredded mozzarella cheese

Directions:

1. Preheat oven to 450 degrees F (230 degrees C).
2. Heat the oil in a skillet over medium heat, and sauté the pepperoni and bacon until evenly browned.
3. Mix in the mushrooms, onion, and green pepper.
4. Cook and stir about 5 minutes, until tender.
5. In a medium saucepan over medium heat, mix the ingredients from the skillet with the tomato sauce and beer.
6. Season with garlic, oregano, thyme, and salt. Allow the mixture to simmer for about 15 minutes, until slightly thickened.
7. Spread over the 2 pizza crusts, and top with cheese.
8. Bake 20 to 25 minutes in the preheated oven, until the cheese is melted and the crust is golden brown.

Bakery-Style Pizza

Dough Ingredients:

1 1/4 cups warm water
1 tsp. active dry yeast
3 cups bread flour
1 1/2 tsps. fine salt
1/4 cup olive oil, divided

Sauce Ingredients:

1 (28 oz.) can plain crushed tomatoes
1 (14 oz.) can pizza sauce

Cheese Ingredients:

8 oz. low-moisture whole-milk mozzarella, very thinly sliced
1/4 cup grated Pecorino Romano cheese

Directions:

1. Combine water and yeast in a small bowl. Let stand until yeast softens and begins to form a creamy foam, about 5 minutes.
2. Combine flour and salt together in the bowl of a stand mixer fitted with a dough hook attachment.
3. Pour in yeast mixture.
4. Knead dough until smooth, about 7 minutes.
5. Grease a large bowl lightly with olive oil. Form dough into a tight ball and lightly grease the top.
6. Place in the bowl; cover loosely with plastic wrap.
7. Let rise until doubled in volume, about 30 minutes.
8. Mix crushed tomatoes and pizza sauce together in a bowl to make sauce.
9. Grease a heavy-gauge rimmed 12x17-inch baking sheet generously with olive oil. Press dough into the bottom. Prick dough all over with a fork.
10. Arrange mozzarella cheese slices over dough; cover with 1 cup sauce.
11. Sprinkle Pecorino Romano cheese on top. Drizzle remaining olive oil over pizza.
12. Let pizza rise in a warm area until puffy, about 1 hour.
13. Preheat oven to 450 degrees F (230 degrees C).
14. Bake pizza on the center rack of the preheated oven until edges are very dark brown but top is not burnt, 15 to 20 minutes.
15. Cool in the pan for 5 minutes before slicing into squares.

Sicilian Pizza Crust

Ingredients:

1 cup warm water (95 to 110 degrees F/35 to 43 degrees C)
1 (.25 oz.) package active dry yeast
2 tbsps. shortening
1 1/2 tsps. salt
1 tsp. white sugar
1 tsp. Italian seasoning
3 cups all-purpose flour

Directions:

1. Combine warm water and yeast in a small bowl; stir until yeast is dissolved. Let stand until yeast forms a creamy foam, about 10 minutes.
2. Pour yeast mixture into a large bowl; add shortening, salt, sugar, and Italian seasoning.
3. Stir in flour by hand until dough comes together.
4. Turn dough out on a floured work surface and knead until smooth, 5 to 8 minutes. Transfer to a large greased bowl.
5. Cover with a moist towel and let rise in a warm place until doubled in size, about 45 minutes.
6. Punch dough down gently. Let stand for 3 to 5 minutes for air to release.
7. Roll into a ball; spread and stretch over the bottom of a pizza pan. Let rise for 15 minutes before topping and baking seasoning.

Thai Chicken Pizza

Ingredients:

1 (12 inch) pre-baked pizza crust
1 (7 oz.) jar peanut sauce
1/4 cup peanut butter
8 oz. cooked skinless, boneless chicken breast halves, cut into strips
1 cup shredded Italian cheese blend
1 bunch green onions, chopped
1/2 cup fresh bean sprouts
1/2 cup shredded carrot (Optional)
1 tbsp. chopped roasted peanuts (Optional)

Directions:

1. Preheat the oven to 400 degrees F (200 degrees C).
2. In a small bowl, stir together the peanut sauce and peanut butter.
3. Spread over the pizza crust.
4. Arrange strips of chicken on top.
5. Sprinkle on the green onions and cheese.
6. Bake for 8 to 12 minutes in the preheated oven, until cheese is melted and bubbly.
7. Top with bean sprouts, carrot shreds and peanuts, if using.
8. Slice into wedges and serve.

Philly Cheese Steak Pizza

Sauce Ingredients:

1 tbsp. butter
1 tbsp. flour
1/2 cup cold milk
1-3 cloves garlic, pressed
1/8 tsp. salt
1 pinch black pepper
1 pinch nutmeg
1/4 cup parmesan cheese

Pizza Ingredients:

1/2 recipe homemade
6 oz. of cooked ribeye, skirt, or flank steak, or roast beef
1/2 green bell pepper, sliced
3-5 mushrooms sliced
1/2 sweet onion, thinly sliced
3 tsps. oil (optional)
1 1/4 cup shredded cheese (such as mozzarella or provolone)

Directions:

1. Position a rack in the center of the oven and preheat the oven to 475 degrees F.
2. Roll the dough out into a 12 inch circle.
3. Create a lip or rim by thickening the dough around the crust portion.
4. Let dough rest for 15-20 minutes while you prepare the sauce.
5. Melt the butter in a small saucepan over medium heat.
6. Whisk in the flour and let cook for 1 minute or until it smells like baked pie dough.
7. Slowly stream in the cold milk while you whisk.
8. Add the pressed garlic and allow the sauce to come to a gentle simmer.
9. Season with salt, pepper, and nutmeg.
10. Remove the sauce from the stove; whisk in the parmesan cheese. Allow the sauce to cool for 5-10 minutes.
11. Top the dough with sauce, cooked steak, veggies, and shredded cheese.
12. Bake for 12-15 minutes or until the crust is lightly browned and the cheese is bubbling and golden.
13. Slice pizza and serve!

Pizza On The Grill

Ingredients:

1 ready made pizza crust
2 cups shredded mozzarella cheese
1 cup tomato sauce
1/2 cup chopped green bell pepper
1/2 cup fresh sliced mushrooms

Directions:

1. Preheat an outdoor grill for high heat and lightly oil grate.
2. Roll out prepared pizza dough to a size that will fit your grill.
3. Place on grill for 5 minutes, or to desired doneness, and flip over. Now add the sauce, cheese, green bell pepper and mushrooms.
4. Cover the grill and allow to cook over high heat for 5 to 10 minutes, or until cheese is melted and bubbly.

No-Yeast Pizza Crust

Ingredients:

1 1/3 cups all-purpose flour
1 tsp. baking powder
1/2 tsp. salt
1/2 cup fat-free milk
2 tbsps. olive oil

Directions:

1. Mix flour, baking powder, and salt together in a bowl; stir in milk and olive oil until a soft dough forms.
2. Turn dough onto a lightly floured surface and knead 10 times. Shape dough into a ball.
3. Cover dough with an inverted bowl and let sit for 10 minutes.
4. Roll dough into a 12-inch circle on a baking sheet.

Maryland Chocolate Crab Pizza

Ingredients:

12 oz. milk chocolate
2 oz. chocolate chips
1-oz. mini marshmallows
1/2 oz. crisped rice cereal
2 oz. white chocolate

Directions:

1. Place a sheet of waxed paper on a cookie sheet.
2. Pour tempered chocolate in circle.
3. Pour chocolate chips, marshmallows and rice cereal on center of chocolate.
4. Hand mix and spread in a 8 to 9-inch circle.
5. Drizzle on white chocolate and add candy crabs of your choice for toppings (m&m's, peanuts, other candies, etc.)
6. Let harden and enjoy.

Cast-Iron Pizza

Ingredients:

1 pound frozen pizza dough, thawed and risen
1/4 cup olive oil
1/2 cup store-bought pizza sauce
1/2 cup pepperoni
4 oz. fresh mozzarella pearls
1/4 cup torn fresh basil

Directions:

1. Place a 12-inch cast-iron skillet in the oven and preheat to 500 degrees F.
2. Meanwhile, roll or stretch the dough into a 14-inch circle.
3. Carefully remove the skillet from the oven.
4. Drizzle two thirds of the olive oil into the skillet, then carefully transfer the dough to the skillet, pressing the dough up the edges.
5. Spread the sauce over the dough, making sure to get all the way to the edges.
6. Shingle the pepperoni over the sauce and top with the mozzarella pearls. Brush the exposed dough with the remaining olive oil.
7. Bake on the bottom rack until golden brown, 12 to 14 minutes.
8. Transfer to a cutting board, top with torn basil, cut into slices and serve.

Chickpea Pizza Crust

Ingredients:

Nonstick cooking spray, for the baking sheet
1 (15-oz.) can chickpeas, rinsed, drained and dried
1 tbsp. gluten-free flour
1 tsp. garlic powder
1 tsp. Italian seasoning
1 tsp. onion powder
1 tsp. kosher salt
1 large egg
Freshly ground black pepper
Desired pizza toppings

Directions:

1. Preheat the oven to 425 degrees F.
2. For the tomato sauce: In a large pot, heat the oil over medium-high heat.
3. Add the garlic, carrots and onion and sauté until the vegetables are soft, approximately 5 minutes.
4. Season with salt and pepper.
5. Add the tomato sauce and bring to a simmer.
6. Cover and simmer on low heat until thick, about 20 minutes.
7. For the crust: Meanwhile, in a bowl, whisk together the chickpea flour, garlic powder, salt and 2/3 cup water.
8. In a 7 1/2-inch round nonstick pan, heat the olive oil over medium heat and pour the "dough" into the pan (about 1/8 inch thick).
9. Cook the "dough" until the edges start to brown, approximately 3 minutes. Flip the crust over like a pancake and cook on the other side for another 3 minutes. Transfer the crust to a baking sheet.
10. To finish the tomato sauce, put the sauce into a food processor and process until smooth.
11. For the pizza topping: Brush the olive oil over the chickpea crust.
12. Spread a thin layer of the tomato sauce over the crust, leaving a 1/2-inch border.
13. Sprinkle on the grated provolone, covering the tomato sauce.
14. Place the chicken sausage slices on top.
15. Bake until the cheese is melted and bubbling, 10 to 15 minutes.

Cauliflower Pizza Crust

Ingredients:

1 head cauliflower, stalk removed
1/2 cup shredded mozzarella
1/4 cup grated Parmesan
1/2 tsp. dried oregano
1/2 tsp. kosher salt
1/4 tsp. garlic powder
2 eggs, lightly beaten

Directions:

1. Preheat the oven to 400 degrees F. Line a baking sheet with parchment paper.
2. Break the cauliflower into florets and pulse in a food processor until fine.
3. Steam in a steamer basket and drain well. (I like to put it on a towel to get all the moisture out.) Let cool.
4. In a bowl, combine the cauliflower with the mozzarella, Parmesan, oregano, salt, garlic powder and eggs. Transfer to the center of the baking sheet and spread into a circle, resembling a pizza crust.
5. Bake for 20 minutes.
6. Add desired toppings and bake an additional 10 minutes.

Sicilian Meatball Pizza

Roasted Pepper Honey Ingredients:

1 large red bell pepper
1/2 cup honey
2 tbsps. extra-virgin olive oil
1/2 tsp. crushed red pepper flakes, optional
Kosher salt

Pizza Ingredients:

2 tsps. olive oil, plus more for drizzling
1 (18-oz.) ball pizza dough, at room temperature
1/2 cup marinara sauce, at room temperature
3 to 4 oz. low-moisture mozzarella, sliced
6 medium fully cooked and cooled meatballs, recipe follows
8 leaves fresh basil, roughly torn
5 tbsps. finely grated Pecorino Romano
1 tbsp. Sicilian (or regular dried) oregano

Meatballs Ingredients:

4 to 5 slices white bread (about 5 oz.), torn into small chunks
1/2 cup whole milk
Kosher salt and freshly ground black pepper
4 oz. ground beef
4 oz. ground pork
4 oz. ground veal
2 to 4 oz. freshly grated pecorino
3 cloves garlic, grated
1 large egg
1/2 bunch fresh parsley, chopped (about 1/2 cup)

Directions:

1. Preheat the oven to 500 degrees F.
2. For the pizza: Grease the bottom of a 13-by-9-inch rimmed baking sheet with the oil.
3. Use your fingers to spread and stretch the dough super thin to fill the baking sheet.
4. Cover with a clean towel or plastic wrap and let sit at room temperature until the dough is slightly puffed, about 1 hour.
5. For the roasted pepper honey:
6. Place the pepper over an open flame over high heat.
7. Roast, using tongs to turn on all sides, until completely black, 2 to 3 minutes per side.
8. Transfer the pepper to a paper bag (or to a large bowl covered with plastic), fold the bag closed and steam, about 10 minutes.

9. Transfer the pepper to a cutting board, cut in half and scrape out and discard the seeds. Turn the pepper over and use a kitchen towel to wipe the charred skin from the outside (do not rinse).
10. Add the pepper, honey, oil, crushed red pepper flakes if using and salt to taste to a blender and blend until smooth.
11. Set aside or keep in a glass jar with a lid in the refrigerator up to 2 weeks.
12. Makes about 1 cup.
13. Gently spread the tomato sauce on top of the dough, then top with the mozzarella. Break the meatballs into small pieces and layer on top of the pizza.
14. Sprinkle with half the basil and drizzle with olive oil.
15. Top with half the pecorino and the oregano.
16. Bake until crisped and browned, 4 to 5 minutes.
17. Remove the baking sheet from the oven and place it on the stove over medium heat to gently fry the bottom of the pizza until crisp, 1 to 2 minutes.
18. Sprinkle with the remaining basil and drizzle with about 1 tbsp. of the roasted pepper honey and additional olive oil.
19. Sprinkle with the remaining pecorino, slice the hot pizza and serve immediately.

Meatballs Directions:

1. Combine the bread, milk and pepper to taste in a large bowl and mix with your hands until a paste forms.
2. Add the beef, pork, veal, pecorino, garlic, egg, parsley and a pinch each salt and pepper, then use your hands to gently combine.
3. Heat 2 tbsps. of the oil in a large skillet over medium heat.
4. Scoop about six 1-inch chunks of the meatball mixture into the skillet and cook, turning occasionally, until all sides are browned, 6 to 7 minutes total. Use a slotted spoon to transfer the meatballs to a kitchen towel or plate and let cool completely, about 1 hour.
5. Repeat with the remaining oil and meatball mixture or freeze:
6. Arrange the remaining uncooked meatballs in a single layer on a baking sheet and freeze until solid.
7. Transfer the frozen uncooked meatballs to a freezer bag or freezer-safe container and store up to 2 months.
8. Makes 20 meatballs.

About the Author

Laura Sommers is **The Recipe Lady!**

She lives on a small farm in Baltimore County, Maryland and has a passion for all things domestic especially when it comes to saving money. She has a profitable eBay business and is a couponing addict. Follow her tips and tricks to learn how to make delicious meals on a budget, save money or to learn the latest life hack!

Visit my Amazon Author Page to see my latest books:

amazon.com/author/laurasommers

Visit my blog for even more great recipes:

http://the-recipe-lady.blogspot.com/

Follow me on Pinterest:

http://pinterest.com/therecipelady1

Follow me on Facebook:

https://www.facebook.com/therecipegirl/

Follow me on Twitter:

https://twitter.com/TheRecipeLady1

Other Books by Laura Sommers

Lobster Cookbook

Shrimp Cookbook

Catfish Cookbook

Tuna Fish Salad Recipes